LEE BAILEY'S
Portable Food

Lee Bailey's
Portable Food

PHOTOGRAPHS BY TOM ECKERLE

CLARKSON POTTER/PUBLISHERS
NEW YORK

My sincerest thanks to the people at Lechters, Inc., for supplying the wide selection of containers pictured here, as well as all the kitchen equipment and utensils. And with special thanks to Julie Trela of N. W. Ayer. And, also—Tom Eckerle, James Lartin, Lee Klein, Francine Maroukian, Sibby Lynch, Tom Booth, Sherry Jo Williams, Mardee and Gary Regan, Jim Lillis, Helen Skor.

. . . .

Published by Clarkson N. Potter Inc., 201 East 50th Street, New York, New York 10022. Member of the Crown Publishing Group.

Random House, Inc. New York, Toronto, London, Sydney, Auckland

CLARKSON N. POTTER, POTTER, and colophon are trademarks of Clarkson N. Potter, Inc.

Manufactured in China

DESIGN BY RENATO STANISIC

Library of Congress Cataloging-in-Publication Data is available upon request
ISBN 0-517-59750-0
10 9 8 7 6 5 4 3 2 1
First Edition

Contents

· · · · · · · · · · · · ·

Introduction

. . . .

Beginning about twenty-five years ago, I got into the habit of escaping to the warmth of the Caribbean each winter. It began with short hops, but over time the stays grew longer. In those days, ports like Marigot on the French side of St. Martin still dozed at midday, and planes making the heart-stopping approach to nearby St. Bart's were guided in from an ancient station wagon parked rakishly by the grassy runway. On one of my very first trips down there we decided to find a boat to take us fishing. Two days later, at the crack of dawn, we found ourselves climbing aboard a rather tired-looking craft. The Dutch couple we hired it from had assured us everything we would need, including lunch, would be provided. Of course, we had barely reached open water before we all were ravenously hungry. The skipper's wife went below and was back in a blink with Dutch cheese, delicious home-canned red onion slices, grainy mustard, and bread from the local bakery, almost literally fresh from the oven. So with the tarp flapping overhead, we enjoyed hefty chunks of the bread spread with mustard, topped with generous slices of ham and cheese, and finished off with a slice of onion. I remember to this day how satisfying that simple meal was.

This penchant I have for renting other people's vacation houses got rolling on that trip, and it has persisted to this day. It is in part responsible for my writing this book. It seems I was constantly making food to bring places—not just to vacation houses but also to picnics on the beach or concerts at Tanglewood. Looking back, I am astonished at the variety of food that was appropriate to all these situations.

So on the following pages you will find my suggestions for packable, make-ahead foods that can survive the trip, be it a long plane ride, a lunch in the office, or simply a walk to the shade of a back-yard tree. There are even all-in-one dinners that simply require reheating and a salad to make them table-ready.

I must offer sincere thanks to the Earl of Sandwich, who supposedly gave his name, as well as his stamp of approval, to the first known, really portable food. And to the fabled Marquis de Cookie, for his contribution to the genre, I acknowledge a great debt. (Efforts to verify the marquis's lineage, indeed his actual existence, proved fruitless. Many scholars have even gone so far as to suggest that the marquis may have been a "fig new-ton" of some early culinary prankster's overheated imagination.)

These gentlemen notwithstanding, to my way of Southern thinking, portable food really all began in a cast-iron skillet when the first chicken was fried in hog fat. It seems appropriate to begin this book not with some sandwich or cookie but with my version of my favorite portable food.

A new take on a classic: Southern Fried Pecan Chicken fingers.

Southern Fried Pecan Chicken

2 pounds boneless, skinless chicken breasts
1¹⁄₂ cups buttermilk
2 cups pecans
1¹⁄₃ cups flour
1¹⁄₂ teaspoons salt
¹⁄₂ teaspoon black pepper
Olive oil, for frying

Cut each chicken breast lengthwise into 4 strips. Place the chicken in a bowl, cover with the buttermilk, and marinate for 30 minutes.

Place all the dry ingredients into the bowl of a food processor. Pulse the mixture until the nuts are roughly chopped. Place this mixture into a bowl. Dip the chicken pieces into the nut mixture, pressing it onto the chicken to coat it well. Set the coated pieces on a plate, cover with plastic wrap, and refrigerate for at least 30 minutes.

Fill a cast-iron skillet half way with oil and heat over medium-high heat until hot, not smoking. Drop in chicken and cook on each side until golden brown, approximately 4 minutes per side. Drain the chicken on paper towels.

Serves 6

Simp

The soups I've chosen for this book are all light, which is the way I like them. Any one of them could be the main event for a quick and easy lunch. You may, however, easily expand your menu by adding something like Ham and Cheese Muffins (page 18) or Onion Parmesan Breadsticks

le Soups

(page 16). Of course, should you want dessert, there are always cookies.

I want to point out that soups don't necessarily need to be served piping hot to be good. As a matter of fact, I like some better served at just above room temperature, as many Italians serve them.

Spring Soup

Eminently portable, but don't keep this too long, as the lettuce should look fresh.

2 tablespoons unsalted butter

1½ cups coarsely chopped leeks (white part only)

⅓ cup sliced shallots

⅓ cup sliced scallions

¾ cup grated carrots

4 cups roughly chopped romaine lettuce

¾ cup small peas (fresh or frozen)

5 cups chicken stock

1 cup cooked rice

¾ teaspoon salt

¼ teaspoon black pepper

Melt the butter in a large saucepan over medium-high heat. Add the leeks and cook, stirring occasionally, until just beginning to brown, approximately 10 minutes. Add the shallots and stir. Cover and cook for 2 minutes. Add the scallions, carrots, lettuce, and peas. Stir to combine and cook, covered, for 3 minutes. Add the stock and cook, covered, for 5 minutes. Add the rice and stir to combine. Add the salt and pepper and adjust seasoning if necessary.

Serves 6

Summer Tomato Soup

Make sure to string the celery before you chop it.

2 tablespoons olive oil

2 cups finely diced onions

½ cup finely diced green bell pepper

Generous ⅓ cup roughly chopped celery

1½ pounds tomatoes (about 5 medium), peeled,
  seeded, and roughly chopped

2 cups chicken stock

½ teaspoon salt

¼ teaspoon black pepper

1 tablespoon tarragon vinegar

Place the oil in a large, heavy cast-iron skillet. Heat over medium-high heat until hot. Add the onions and sauté for 5 minutes, stirring occasionally. Add the bell pepper and celery. Stir to combine, cover, and cook for 5 minutes, stirring occasionally. Add the tomatoes and stir. Increase the heat to high and cook for 5 minutes, until the tomatoes give up their juice and become tender. Add the stock, salt, and pepper and stir. Heat the soup thoroughly; there's no need to boil it. Add the vinegar just before serving.

Serves 4

Opposite: *Spring Soup.* Below: *Summer Tomato Soup.*

Potato and Red Pepper Soup

1 tablespoon unsalted butter

1 small onion, roughly chopped

2 garlic cloves, minced

4 cups chicken stock

2 large baking potatoes, peeled and each cut into
    8 pieces

1 large red bell pepper, roasted, peeled, and seeded

1 teaspoon salt

¼ teaspoon black pepper

Melt the butter in a saucepan over medium-high heat. Add the onion and cook, covered, until just starting to brown, approximately 7 minutes. Add the garlic and cook, stirring constantly, for 1 minute. Add the chicken stock and the potatoes. Bring to a boil. Cover, reduce the heat, and simmer until the potatoes are tender, approximately 20 minutes. Stir in the bell pepper.

Allow the soup to cool slightly, then puree it in batches in a food processor. Strain the puree and season with salt and pepper.

Serves 6

BELOW: *Potato and Red Pepper Soup.* OPPOSITE: *Beet, Carrot, and Sweet Potato Soup.*

Beet, Carrot, and Sweet Potato Soup

½ pound beets

½ pound sweet potatoes (2 medium)

1 large yellow onion

4 shallots

4 garlic cloves

1 pound carrots, scraped and roughly chopped

4 cups chicken stock

¼ cup buttermilk

1 teaspoon fresh lemon juice

½ teaspoon salt

¼ teaspoon black pepper

1 cup frozen petit pois, rinsed well under hot water

Preheat the oven to 400 degrees.

Wrap the beets in foil and place them in the oven with the sweet potatoes. Roast until tender, about 1½ hours for the beets and 1 hour for the sweet potatoes, depending on size. Remove from the oven and allow to cool.

Peel and quarter the onion, shallots, and garlic. Combine them with the carrots and stock in a saucepan and cook, covered, over medium heat until the carrots are tender, about 20 minutes. Set aside to cool slightly.

Peel the beets and sweet potatoes and combine them with the cooled soup. Puree the mixture in batches in a food processor and strain back into the saucepan. Stir in the buttermilk, lemon juice, salt, pepper, and petit pois. Warm thoroughly.

Serves 6 to 8

Breads &

The breadsticks, cloverleaf rolls, ham and cheese muffins, and bacon and corn muffins are all delicious eaten on their own or as an accompaniment to soups or salads. As for the sweet muffins, once you taste them

Muffins

I'm sure you will know exactly what to do with them.

All of these can be made in advance and can even be frozen if you like. They're all tender enough to be delicious and sturdy enough to be packed and transported.

Parmesan Breadsticks

゜ yellow onion, chopped
2 tablespoons olive oil
1³/₄ teaspoons active dry yeast
1¹/₄ cups warm (105–115 degrees) water
1 tablespoon molasses
2 tablespoons solid vegetable shortening, melted
3³/₄ cups all-purpose flour
1 teaspoon salt
¹/₂ cup grated Parmesan cheese

Sauté the onion in the olive oil over medium heat until golden brown, about 10 to 12 minutes. Set aside to cool.

Sprinkle the yeast over the water in a small bowl. Add the molasses and the melted shortening; stir to combine. Set aside to proof until frothy, 6 to 8 minutes.

Place the flour and salt in the bowl of a food processor. Pulse once or twice to combine. Pour the yeast mixture into the machine while it is running, and process until the dough forms a ball. Remove to a floured board and add the reserved onion and the grated cheese. Knead by hand for several minutes, adding more flour if needed, until the dough is smooth and elastic.

Roll out the dough into a large rectangle, approximately 12 × 4 inches. Brush the dough with additional oil and cover with a dish towel. Set aside in a warm place until doubled in size, about 1 hour.

Preheat the oven to 450 degrees. Cut the dough into 24 equal pieces. Roll each breadstick with your hands until it is 10 or 12 inches long. Place on a cookie sheet and bake until golden brown, 10 to 12 minutes.

Makes 24 breadsticks

Cloverleaf Rolls

¹/₄ cup instant mashed potato flakes
2 cups milk, scalded
1 package (1 scant tablespoon) active dry yeast
¹/₂ cup warm (105–115 degrees) water
Pinch of sugar
6 cups bread flour
1 tablespoon salt
4 tablespoons unsalted butter, melted and cooled
White cornmeal

Place the instant potatoes in a small bowl. Add the scalded milk and stir to dissolve. In another bowl, combine the yeast, water, and sugar. Stir well and set aside to proof until frothy, 6 to 8 minutes.

In the bowl of a heavy-duty electric mixer fitted with a dough hook, combine the flour and salt, then add the potato mixture, yeast mixture, and butter. Stir with a rubber spatula until the flour is moistened. Work the dough at medium speed with the dough hook for 10 minutes. It should form a ball and pull away from the bottom of the bowl. Place the dough in a clean, lightly oiled bowl. Cover with a clean dish towel and set aside in a warm place to rise until doubled in volume, about 1 hour.

Lightly butter the insides of 24 large muffin cups. Sprinkle a small amount of the cornmeal in the cups and rotate to evenly coat the interiors.

Punch the dough down; break off small pieces and roll them into small balls. Place 3 small balls of dough into each buttered muffin tin. Cover loosely with plastic wrap and set aside in a warm place to rise until almost doubled, about 1 hour.

Preheat the oven to 375 degrees.

Bake the rolls for 35 to 40 minutes or until golden brown. Remove the rolls from the muffin tins and allow to cool on a wire rack.

Makes 24 large rolls

ABOVE: *Onion Parmesan Breadsticks.* BELOW: *Cloverleaf Rolls.*

d Cheese Muffins

...pose flour
1 tablespoon baking powder
½ teaspoon salt
1 egg, at room temperature
1 cup buttermilk, at room temperature
¼ cup canola oil
8 ounces boneless ham steak, cut into small dice
1¼ cups grated sharp Cheddar cheese

Preheat the oven to 450 degrees. Lightly grease and flour 12 large muffin tins (or line them with paper liners).

In a large bowl, stir together the flour, baking powder, and salt. Set aside.

Whisk together the egg, buttermilk, and oil in a small bowl. Stir in the ham and cheese. Using a rubber spatula, stir the egg mixture into the dry ingredients just until combined. Do not overmix. Use a ladle to fill each of the prepared muffin tins approximately two-thirds full. Place in the oven and lower the temperature to 400 degrees. Bake until golden brown, about 20 minutes.

Makes 12 large muffins

Variations

BACON AND CHEESE MUFFINS Substitute 6 slices thick-cut bacon for the ham. Dice the bacon and sauté it in a heavy skillet over medium-high heat until it is just crisp. Do not overcook it. Drain on paper towels and allow to cool. Combine the bacon and cheese with the egg mixture and continue as above.

SAUSAGE AND CHEESE MUFFINS Substitute 8 ounces Italian sausage (hot or sweet) for the ham. Remove the sausage from the casing and sauté it in a heavy skillet over medium-high heat until completely cooked. Drain on paper towels and allow to cool. If necessary, roughly chop the cooked sausage with a knife. Mix the sausage and cheese with the egg mixture and continue as above.

. . . .

Bacon and Onion Corn Muffins

6 strips thick-cut bacon, diced
1½ cups diced onions
1 cup buttermilk, at room temperature
½ cup plus 2 tablespoons yellow cornmeal
2¼ cups all-purpose flour
1 teaspoon baking soda
2 teaspoons baking powder
4 tablespoons unsalted butter, softened
4 tablespoons vegetable shortening, softened
2 eggs

Preheat the oven to 400 degrees. Lightly grease and flour 12 large muffin tins (or line them with paper liners).

Sauté the bacon in a heavy skillet over medium-high heat until golden brown and just crisp. Do not overcook. Use a slotted spoon to

OPPOSITE: *Ham and Cheese Muffins.* ABOVE: *Bacon and Onion Corn Muffins.*

remove the bacon to paper towels. Reserve the fat and set the bacon aside to cool. Sauté the onions in the bacon fat over medium-high heat until light brown, 8 to 10 minutes. Place the onions in a strainer set over a bowl and allow the fat to drain out.

In a small bowl, combine the buttermilk with ½ cup of cornmeal and stir well. Set aside. In a separate bowl, whisk together the remaining cornmeal with the flour, baking soda, and baking powder. Set aside.

Cream the butter and shortening with an electric mixer in a large bowl until light. Add the eggs one at a time, mixing well after each addition. On low speed, stir in the buttermilk mixture and mix until just combined. Slowly add the flour mixture and stir on low speed until the mixture is just combined. Do not overmix. Scrape down the sides and

bottom of the bowl with a rubber scraper and stir in the onions and the bacon until just combined.

Fill the muffin tins two-thirds full. Place in the oven and reduce heat to 350 degrees. Bake for 20 to 25 minutes, until golden brown. Test to see if the muffins are done by inserting a toothpick into the center of one of the muffins; it should be clean when removed. Cool on a rack.

Makes 12 large muffins

Variations

HAM CORN MUFFINS Replace the bacon and onions with 12 ounces diced ham.

HAM AND CHEESE CORN MUFFINS Replace the bacon and onions with 8 ounces finely diced ham and 1¼ cups grated sharp Cheddar cheese.

Dried Strawberry Cherry Muffins

1 cup dried strawberries
1 cup dried cherries
$^{1}/_{2}$ cup boiling water
2 cups all-purpose flour
$^{1}/_{2}$ teaspoon ground cinnamon
2 teaspoons baking powder
1 teaspoon baking soda
$^{1}/_{2}$ teaspoon salt
$^{2}/_{3}$ cup sugar
2 eggs, lightly beaten
$^{1}/_{3}$ cup unsalted butter, melted and cooled

Preheat the oven to 400 degrees. Grease and lightly flour 12 standard muffin cups (or line them with paper liners).

Put the strawberries and cherries in a heatproof bowl and pour in the boiling water. Set aside until cool.

Stir together the flour, cinnamon, baking powder, baking soda, salt, and sugar in a large bowl.

Stir the eggs and butter into the strawberries and cherries. Using a large rubber spatula, stir the egg-fruit mixture into the flour mixture and stir until just blended. Do not overmix.

Fill the muffin cups two-thirds full. Place in the oven and reduce heat to 350 degrees. Bake for 25 minutes, or until a cake tester comes out clean.

Makes 12 muffins

Variation

DRIED BLUEBERRY CHERRY MUFFINS
Substitute 1 cup dried blueberries for the dried strawberries. The blueberries don't need to be soaked; simply fold them in after you add the cherries.

Raisin Bran Muffins

3 cups raisin bran cereal
$^1/_2$ cup raisins
1 cup hot black coffee
$2^1/_2$ cups all-purpose flour
1 cup sugar
$2^1/_2$ teaspoons baking soda
2 eggs, lightly beaten
$^1/_2$ cup unsalted butter, melted and cooled
2 cups buttermilk

Preheat the oven to 400 degrees. Grease and lightly flour 24 standard muffin cups (or line them with paper liners).

Place the cereal and raisins in a large bowl. Pour in the hot coffee and stir to combine. Set aside.

Whisk together the flour, sugar, and baking soda in a large mixing bowl. Set aside.

Stir the eggs, butter, and buttermilk into the cereal mixture. Add this to the flour mixture and stir with a rubber spatula until just combined. Do not overmix. Fill the prepared muffin tins two-thirds full. Bake for 18 to 20 minutes, until a cake tester comes out clean.

Makes 24 muffins

OPPOSITE: *Dried Strawberry Cherry Muffins.*
ABOVE: *Raisin Bran Muffins.* RIGHT: *Applesauce Currant Muffins.*

Applesauce Curra

$^1/_2$ cup unsalted butter, softened
1 cup sugar
1 cup applesauce (preferably home
$^1/_2$ teaspoon vanilla extract
$1^1/_2$ cups all-purpose flour
$^1/_2$ teaspoon ground cinnamon
$^1/_2$ teaspoon freshly grated nutmeg
$^1/_4$ teaspoon ground mace
1 teaspoon baking soda
1 cup walnuts, coarsely chopped
$^1/_2$ cup currants

Preheat the oven to 400 degrees. Grease and lightly flour 15 muffin tins (or line them with paper liners).

Using an electric mixer, cream the butter and sugar in a large bowl until light. Fold in the applesauce and the vanilla. The mixture will look curdled. Set aside.

Whisk together the flour, cinnamon, nutmeg, mace, and baking soda. Remove 2 tablespoons of the flour mixture and dredge the nuts and currants until they are well coated. Set aside. Using a large rubber spatula, fold the flour mixture into the butter-sugar mixture. Stir just to combine; do not overmix. Stir in the nuts and currants.

Fill the tins two-thirds full and bake for 25 minutes, or until a cake tester comes out clean.

Makes 15 muffins

Muffins

Use your favorite jam to fill these.

2½ cups all-purpose flour
1 teaspoon baking soda
2 teaspoons baking powder
1¼ cups packed brown sugar
⅔ cup canola oil
2 eggs, lightly beaten
1 cup buttermilk
6 tablespoons jam
½ cup sliced almonds

Preheat the oven to 400 degrees. Grease and lightly flour 18 muffin tins (or line them with paper liners).

In a medium bowl, whisk together the flour, baking soda, and baking powder. Set aside.

Combine the sugar, oil, and eggs in a large mixing bowl. Stir well with a large rubber spatula. Add the buttermilk and stir to combine. Stir the dry ingredients into the wet until just combined. Do not overmix.

Fill the muffin tins two-thirds full. Place 1 teaspoon of jam in the center of each muffin. Surround the jam with sliced almonds. Place in the oven and reduce heat to 350 degrees. Bake until golden brown, about 20 minutes.

Makes 18 muffins

Jam Muffins are topped with slivered almonds.

Side-Di

sh Salads

I'm sure that you will find plenty of uses for these. Almost any of them would enhance a luncheon menu, and many times I serve a combination of salads as the entire meal.

As with any salad, the quantities may be altered to suit your personal taste. Feel free to adjust them as you like.

Green Bean and Cheese Salad

14 ounces green beans, cut into 1-inch pieces
1 cup grated Gruyère cheese
4 ounces (about 8 large) shallots, minced
2 tablespoons olive oil
2 tablespoons red wine vinegar
1 tablespoon grainy Dijon mustard
$1/4$ teaspoon salt
$1/8$ teaspoon black pepper

Blanch the green beans in boiling salted water for 5 minutes. Drain and run under cold water to stop the cooking. Drain well, then combine with the cheese in a large mixing bowl.

Whisk together all remaining ingredients for dressing. Combine with the green beans and cheese. Mix well.

Serves 6

. . . .

Beet Salad

3 small onions
1 tablespoon olive oil
1 tablespoon balsamic vinegar
Salt and black pepper
2 pounds beets

DRESSING
1 tablespoon raspberry vinegar
1 tablespoon balsamic vinegar
2 tablespoons olive oil
$1/2$ teaspoon salt
$1/4$ teaspoon black pepper

Preheat the oven to 400 degrees.

Peel the onions and cut into quarters. Drizzle 1 teaspoon each of the oil and vinegar on each onion. Sprinkle with salt and pepper to taste. Wrap each onion in aluminum foil and twist at the top to seal. Place the beets on a foil-lined baking sheet. Bake until tender, about 1 hour for the onions and $1\frac{1}{2}$ hours for the beets. Set aside to cool. Reserve any liquid for the dressing.

Peel the beets and cut into $1/4$-inch slices, then into thick sticks. Place in a large mixing bowl. Break up the quartered onions and add them to the beets.

To make the dressing, whisk the ingredients together, along with any reserved liquid from the onions. Pour the dressing over the salad and toss.

Serves 6

OPPOSITE: *Green Bean and Cheese Salad.* ABOVE: *Beet Salad.*

ABOVE: *Two-Bean Salad.* BELOW: *Roasted Onion and Potato Salad.*

ABOVE: *Wild Rice Salad.* BELOW: *Sautéed Red and Yellow Pepper Salad.*

Two-Bean Salad

2 pounds green beans, stem ends snapped off
1 can (1 pound) kidney beans, drained
1 large red onion, thinly sliced
2 tablespoons sugar
1/4 cup vegetable oil
3 tablespoons white vinegar
1/4 teaspoon salt
1/4 teaspoon black pepper

Cook the green beans in lightly salted boiling water until tender, approximately 12 minutes. Drain and run under cold water until cool. Drain again and pat dry.

In a large mixing bowl, combine the green beans with the kidney beans and the red onion. In a small bowl, combine the sugar, oil, vinegar, salt, and pepper. Stir to mix well and dissolve the sugar. Add the dressing to the beans and toss to mix.

Serves 6

. . . .

Roasted Onion and Potato Salad

1 tablespoon olive oil
2 teaspoons balsamic vinegar
1 teaspoon Dijon mustard
1 tablespoon chopped parsley
1/4 teaspoon salt
1/4 teaspoon black pepper
3 medium onions
2 pounds small red new potatoes

Preheat the oven to 400 degrees.

Place the oil, vinegar, mustard, parsley, salt, and pepper in a jar with a tight-fitting lid. Shake well.

Peel and quarter the onions. Place each onion on a large square of aluminum foil. Drizzle about a third of the dressing over the onions and twist the foil to seal the packets. Bake until tender, approximately 1 hour.

Scrub the potatoes and cut them into quarters. Place in a large saucepan and barely cover with cold salted water. Bring to a boil and then reduce heat to a simmer. Cook until fork-tender, approximately 20 minutes. Drain and toss the potatoes with the remaining vinaigrette while they are still warm. Break up the onions and add to the potatoes, along with any liquid in the packets. Toss.

Serves 8

. . . .

Wild Rice Salad

4 3/4 cups water
2/3 cup wild rice
1 teaspoon salt
1 cup basmati rice
1 tablespoon vegetable oil
1 cup frozen petit pois

D R E S S I N G
1/4 cup olive oil
1 tablespoon grainy Dijon mustard
1 tablespoon sherry vinegar
3 tablespoons mayonnaise
1/2 teaspoon salt
1/4 teaspoon black pepper

1 medium red bell pepper, roasted, peeled, seeded, and
    coarsely chopped
1 cup finely chopped scallions
1/4 cup diced dill pickle

Bring 3 cups of water to a boil. Add the wild rice and ½ teaspoon salt. Bring back to the boil, reduce the heat to a simmer, and cook for approximately 50 minutes, until the rice has expanded and is tender. Drain the rice and set aside to cool completely.

Bring the remaining 1¾ cups of water to a boil. Add the basmati rice, oil, and ½ teaspoon of salt. Return to a boil, reduce the heat, and cover. Cook for 15 minutes. Remove from heat and fluff the rice with a fork. Allow to cool completely.

Defrost the frozen peas by placing them in a small bowl of warm water. Allow to sit for several minutes until soft and tender. Drain.

To make the dressing, combine the ingredients in a jar with a tight-fitting lid. Shake until well combined.

In a large mixing bowl, combine the wild and basmati rices, the petit pois, red bell pepper, scallions, and pickle. Toss. Add the dressing and mix well.

Serves 6 generously

. . . .

Sautéed Red and Yellow Pepper Salad

Cut the peppers for this salad into slices about 2 inches long and ¼ inch thick.

1 tablespoon olive oil
1½ cups sliced red bell peppers
1½ cups sliced yellow bell peppers
1 tablespoon capers, drained
2 ounces Niçoise olives, pitted and roughly chopped
2 tablespoons balsamic vinegar

Place the olive oil into a very large skillet and heat over high heat. Add the peppers and sauté until just tender, about 3 or 4 minutes, shaking or stirring constantly.

Remove sautéed peppers to a bowl. Add the capers, olives, and balsamic vinegar. Toss to mix.

Serves 6

. . . .

Thai-Style Salad

3 medium cucumbers, peeled, seeded, and sliced
2 medium carrots, peeled and grated
4 large shallots, sliced
½ red onion, sliced
1 small red chili, minced
¾ cup rice vinegar
¼ cup plus 2 tablespoons sugar
3 tablespoons finely chopped cilantro
½ cup peanuts, roughly chopped

Combine the cucumbers, carrots, shallots, onion, and chili in a bowl.

Place the vinegar and sugar in a small saucepan. Bring to a boil and then reduce heat to a simmer. Simmer uncovered for 5 minutes, until the mixture is syrupy. Allow to cool.

Pour the sweetened vinegar over the vegetables and toss. Add the cilantro and peanuts and toss again.

Serves 6

Thai-Style Salad.

at Loaves

Whoever had the notion of making the first meat loaf sure started something. Versions of them are still the mainstay of many diets. Made properly, they are both packable, portable, and tasty. They are also a fine way to use both leftover meats and vegetables. I have been making versions of the ones included here for years, and I seem never to cease to tinker with them.

ABOVE: *Ham Loaf.* OPPOSITE: *Rice Loaf.*

Ham Loaf

2 tablespoons olive oil

1 boneless ham steak (about 13 ounces), cut into
 ¼ × ½-inch strips

1 tablespoon water

1 cup chopped celery

1 cup chopped onion

2 eggs

1 cup milk

1 tablespoon Dijon mustard

½ teaspoon black pepper

2 cups fresh bread crumbs

Preheat the oven to 350 degrees and lightly grease an 8½ × 4½-inch loaf pan.

Heat 1 tablespoon of the olive oil in a large,

heavy skillet over medium-high heat until hot. Add the ham and sauté until it begins to brown, 5 to 10 minutes. Remove from the pan and cut into small pieces. Place in a large mixing bowl.

Add the water and the celery to the pan you cooked the ham in and bring to a boil. Scrape the bottom of the pan with the back of a wooden spoon to dissolve any browned bits. Cook until the water has completely evaporated. Add the onion and the remaining tablespoon of olive oil to the pan and cook until they begin to caramelize, 10 to 12 minutes. Add this mixture to the chopped ham.

Combine the eggs, milk, mustard, and pepper in a medium bowl. Add this mixture and the bread crumbs to the ham mixture. Stir to combine. Pour into the pan and bake for 45 minutes.

Serves 4

Rice Loaf

1½ cups water

⅓ cup basmati rice

⅓ cup bulgur

5 tablespoons unsalted butter

1 medium onion, finely chopped

1 cup finely chopped parsley

2 tablespoons finely chopped canned jalapeño peppers

1 jar (4 ounces) mild green chilies, chopped

2 cups grated sharp Cheddar cheese

1 cup milk

2 eggs

Preheat the oven to 350 degrees and lightly grease an 8½ × 4½-inch loaf pan.

Bring ½ cup water to a boil in a small saucepan. Add the rice, cover, and simmer over low heat for 15 minutes. Set aside to cool.

Meanwhile, bring the remaining 1 cup water to a boil in a separate saucepan. Add the bulgur and stir. Cover and simmer over low heat for 10 minutes. Remove from the heat and leave covered for 15 minutes. Drain if necessary. Set aside to cool.

Melt 1 tablespoon of the butter in a small cast-iron skillet over medium-high heat. Once the pan is hot, add the onion and sauté, stirring occasionally, until it just begins to brown, about 6 or 7 minutes. Remove from the heat, add the parsley, and stir.

In a large mixing bowl, combine the rice, bulgur, jalapeño peppers, green chilies, and sautéed onion and parsley. Stir to combine. Add the cheese and mix well.

Melt the remaining 4 tablespoons butter and combine with the milk and eggs. Add this to the rice mixture and stir.

Spoon the mixture into the pan and bake for 45 to 50 minutes, until golden brown.

Serves 4

Preheat the oven to 350 degrees and lightly grease a 9 × 5-inch loaf pan.

Cut the tomato into wedges, place on a plate, and drizzle with 1 teaspoon olive oil. Place in the microwave and cook on high for 3 minutes. Set aside.

In a medium skillet, heat 2 tablespoons olive oil over medium-high heat until hot, not smoking. Sauté the shallots and celery until just wilted, approximately 3 minutes. Add the garlic and sauté another minute. Remove from heat and allow to cool slightly.

In a large bowl, use your hands to combine and mix the ground meats. In a separate bowl, combine the eggs, Worcestershire sauce, mustard, thyme, salt, and pepper. Beat lightly with a fork and add to the meat mixture. Mix well. (Your hands work best for this.) Add the bread crumbs and mix again.

Spoon the mixture into the pan and arrange the tomato slices and bay leaves on top. Place the pan onto a baking sheet to catch any liquid that may spill over. Bake until golden brown, approximately 1 hour.

Serves 6

. . . .

Meat Loaf

1 medium tomato

2 tablespoons plus 1 teaspoon olive oil

1½ cups finely chopped shallots

1½ cups finely chopped celery

4 large garlic cloves, minced

¾ pound ground beef

¾ pound ground pork

¾ pound ground veal

4 eggs, lightly beaten

2 tablespoons Worcestershire sauce

2 tablespoons Dijon mustard

¾ teaspoon dried thyme

1 teaspoon salt

¾ teaspoon black pepper

2 cups fresh bread crumbs

2 bay leaves

Chicken Loaf

1½ pounds boneless and skinless chicken breast

2 tablespoons olive oil

¾ cup finely chopped onion

¾ cup finely chopped shallots

3 tablespoons finely chopped parsley

¼ cup milk

1 egg

1 teaspoon dried tarragon

¼ teaspoon dried savory

½ teaspoon salt

¼ teaspoon black pepper

1 cup fresh bread crumbs

OPPOSITE: *Meat Loaf.* ABOVE: *Chicken Loaf.*

Preheat the oven to 375 degrees and lightly grease an 8½ × 4½-inch loaf pan.

Cut the chicken breast into chunks, then place in the bowl of a food processor. Pulse until finely chopped. Do not overwork. Place the chicken into a large mixing bowl.

Heat the olive oil in a large cast-iron skillet over medium-high heat until hot, not smoking. Add the onion and shallots and sauté until tender, 6 to 8 minutes. Remove from the heat and stir in the chopped parsley. Allow to cool for several minutes, then add to the chopped chicken.

Combine the milk, egg, tarragon, savory, salt, and pepper in a small bowl. Beat lightly with a fork, then add it to the chicken mixture. Mix by hand. Add the bread crumbs and mix again.

Spoon the mixture into the pan and place it into a deep baking dish. Place the baking dish into the oven and then fill the baking dish with ½ inch of water. Bake for 1 hour. Remove from the oven, leaving the loaf pan in the baking dish. Allow to cool for at least ½ hour. Loosen the sides of the loaf by running a sharp knife around the edge. Carefully drain off any excess liquid and then invert the loaf onto a plate to cool further.

Serves 4

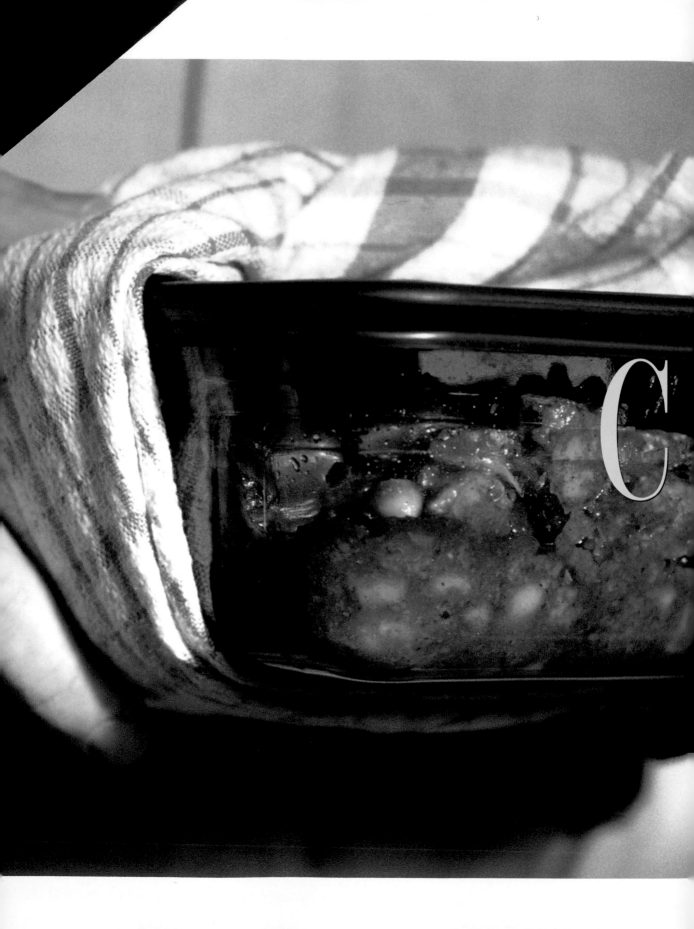

These casseroles are the kind of dishes
that you can make ahead of time
and reheat when you arrive at your
destination. Incidentally, I have found that
a very good way to pack things like
casseroles is to surround them with
unshelled roasted peanuts. These will keep
the casserole intact and the beauty is that

asseroles

that you can then have the peanuts with
drinks before dinner while you're waiting
for the casserole to reheat. You also might
want to tie the casseroles in a dishtowel or
an oversized napkin to catch any spills
during the trip.

   To reheat the casseroles, partially cover
and place in a preheated 350-degree oven
until heated through. Test for heat if you
like by using a meat thermometer.

Oven–Barbecued Sirloin

This casserole is pictured on page 38.

2 pounds sirloin steak
1 teaspoon minced garlic
1 teaspoon salt
1 tablespoon black pepper (preferably freshly ground)
1/2 teaspoon ground ginger
2 bay leaves, crushed
1 can (6 ounces) tomato paste
1/2 cup dark soy sauce
1/4 cup Worcestershire sauce
1/2 cup packed dark brown sugar
1/3 cup flour
1/4 cup olive oil
1 cup chopped onion
1 can (15 ounces) cannellini beans, drained

Preheat the oven to 400 degrees. Trim the meat and cut into 1-inch cubes. Combine the garlic, salt, pepper, ginger, and bay leaves. Rub this mixture all over the meat. Set aside.

In a small saucepan, combine the tomato paste, soy sauce, Worcestershire, and brown sugar. Place over low heat, stirring until the sugar is dissolved. Keep warm.

Dredge the seasoned meat in the flour. Shake off any excess. Add enough olive oil to cover the bottom of a large cast-iron skillet and heat over medium-high heat until the oil is hot but not smoking. Brown the meat on all sides in batches— don't crowd it in the skillet—about 10 minutes per batch. Use a slotted spoon to remove the meat when done. Place in a 2-quart casserole with a tight-fitting lid. If necessary, add more oil to the skillet to brown the remaining meat.

Add the onion to the hot skillet and sauté, stirring occasionally, until tender, 6 to 8 minutes. Spoon the onion over the meat in the casserole and top with the cannellini beans. Add the warm sauce, stir to combine, cover, and bake for 1/2 hours, or until bubbly.

Serves 6

. . . .

Chicken Enchiladas with Andouille Sausage

You can make this with leftover roast chicken.

S A U C E
1/4 cup olive oil
2 1/4 cups roughly chopped onions
1 tablespoon roughly chopped garlic
2 cans (28 ounces each) whole peeled tomatoes
1/2 teaspoon salt
1/2 teaspoon black pepper
1/2 teaspoon dried oregano
1 teaspoon dried basil
1 tablespoon minced canned chipotle chilies

A S S E M B L Y
1 1/2 cups roughly chopped onions
10 10-inch flour tortillas (6 1/2-inch tortillas can be substituted)
2 1/2 cups shredded cooked chicken breast
6 ounces andouille sausage, cut into quarters lengthwise, then into 1/4-inch pieces
1 pound Monterey Jack cheese, grated
1 pound Cheddar cheese, grated
Vegetable oil

To make the sauce, put the olive oil into a large cast-iron skillet, add the onions, and cook over medium-high heat until translucent, about 4 or 5 minutes.

Add the garlic and cook for an additional minute. Add the tomatoes, salt, pepper, oregano, and basil. Bring to a boil, then break up tomatoes with a potato masher. Reduce the heat and simmer for 30 to 40 minutes. Run the sauce through a food mill using the coarse disk. Measure the sauce and if you need to, reduce until you have about 5½ cups. Stir in the chopped chilies. Set aside.

To assemble the casserole, heat a cast-iron skillet over very high heat until hot. Add enough onions to just cover the bottom of the pan. Stir and turn the onions with the edge of a metal spatula for approximately 10 minutes, until well browned. Set aside. Repeat with the remaining onions.

Use a paper towel to lightly oil a skillet with vegetable oil and place it over high heat. Place 1 tortilla in the skillet for several seconds and then flip it and heat the other side. Remove each tortilla as it is heated, stacking them on top of each other until all are done.

Preheat the oven to 350 degrees. Combine the shredded chicken with the andouille sausage. In a large bowl, combine both grated cheeses.

Place ¼ cup sauce, ⅓ cup chicken mixture, 1 tablespoon caramelized onions, and ¼ cup cheese on each tortilla. (If you are using small tortillas, they will be quite full. This is fine.) Roll each tortilla and place it seam side down into a large casserole dish. When all are assembled and lined up in the casserole dish, cover them all with the remaining sauce and the remaining cheese. Bake uncovered for 40 to 45 minutes, until golden brown and bubbly.

Serves 6 to 8

TOP: *Place sauce, chicken mixture, caramelized onions, and cheese on each tortilla.* CENTER: *Roll tortillas.* BOTTOM: *Carefully place tortillas seam side down into casserole dish.*

Venison Sausage and Veal Casserole

Use a light rye bread to make the bread crumbs for this tasty casserole.

13 ounces venison sausage, quartered lengthwise and
    cut into ¼-inch pieces
½ pound boneless veal steak, cut into ½-inch cubes
2 teaspoons salt
2 teaspoons black pepper
⅓ cup flour
6 tablespoons unsalted butter
1 pound mushrooms, roughly chopped
2 cups roughly chopped onions
1 teaspoon minced garlic
2 tablespoons water
16 ounces low-fat sour cream
2 tablespoons Worcestershire sauce
½ teaspoon freshly ground nutmeg
1 cup fresh rye bread crumbs
6 ounces egg noodles, cooked according to package
    directions

Preheat the oven to 375 degrees.

Heat a large cast-iron skillet over medium-high heat. Add the venison sausage and brown it, stirring occasionally. Pour off fat as it accumulates. When brown, remove to a bowl.

Sprinkle the veal pieces with salt and pepper. Dredge in flour and shake off any excess. Heat 1 tablespoon butter over high heat in the skillet that was used for the sausage and brown the veal in batches—do not crowd the meat and use 1 table-spoon butter for each batch of meat. As the meat is browned, remove it from the pan and add to the sausage. Scrape any bits of meat out of the pan and add them to the rest of the meat.

Add 1 tablespoon of butter to the same pan and sauté the mushrooms over high heat until they give up their liquid and reduce slightly, 5 to 7 minutes.

Remove the mushrooms to the bowl with the sausage and veal. Add 1 tablespoon butter to the pan and cook the onions, stirring occasionally, over medium-high heat until translucent, 4 or 5 minutes. Add the garlic and cook an additional minute. Add the 2 tablespoons water to the pan and stir for a minute or so, scraping the bottom of the skillet to deglaze it. Place the onion and garlic mixture in the bowl with the sausage, veal, and mushrooms.

In a small bowl, combine the sour cream, Worcestershire sauce, and nutmeg. Add to the meat mixture and stir to combine.

Sauté the bread crumbs in 1 tablespoon butter until golden brown. Set aside.

Combine the noodles with the sausage and veal mixture. Stir well to combine. Grease a large casserole dish, or spray it with nonstick spray. Place the mixture into the casserole dish and sprinkle the top with the toasted crumbs. Cover with foil or a tight-fitting lid and bake for 45 minutes.

Serves 6

. . . .

Pork Chops and Rice

6 thin boneless pork chops (approximately
2¹⁄₄ pounds)
Salt and black pepper
Flour, for dredging
3 tablespoons olive oil
3 cups diced onions
2 cups chicken stock, heated
2 cups diced green bell peppers
1 cup white rice
Chopped parsley

Preheat the oven to 400 degrees.

Season the pork chops with salt and pepper to taste. Dredge in flour and shake off excess. Heat a large cast-iron skillet over medium-high heat and add 1 tablespoon of the olive oil. Sear the pork chops on both sides until browned, about 1½ minutes per side. Remove the chops to a plate.

Add the remaining 2 tablespoons olive oil to the skillet and then add all of the onions. Cook, stirring from time to time, until translucent, about 5 minutes. Place the onions in the bottom of a large casserole dish that has been greased or sprayed with nonstick spray. Add the stock to the skillet and cook over medium-high heat, stirring occasionally, until it begins to boil. Add the bell peppers and rice to the onions and stir to combine. Once the chicken stock has come to a boil, pour over the rice mixture. Top with the pork chops and bake, covered, for 45 minutes.

Garnish with chopped parsley just before serving.

Serves 6

Opposite: *Venison Sausage and Veal Casserole.*
Below: *Pork Chops and Rice.*

sh Salads

These are twists on old standbys, and I
think they will pique your interest in
them anew. And as was the case with the
casseroles, they all truly require nothing more
than a green salad and dessert to make
a quick and satisfying little lunch or dinner.
If you follow the recipes in this section

carefully, you will get the kinds of results
that I intended when we worked on them,
but remember that these are, after all,
salads, and the quantities are to some degree
arbitrary and certainly personal. So if you
particularly like (or dislike) any of the ingredients, change them to suit your preference.

ABOVE: *Oriental Beef Salad.* BELOW: *Beef Salad.*

ABOVE: *Chipotle Chicken Salad.* BELOW: *Fresh Tuna Salad.*

Oriental Beef Salad

2 teaspoons olive oil
1 beef tenderloin (about 1 pound)
Salt and black pepper
1/4 cup finely chopped scallions

DRESSING
1 1/2 teaspoons soy sauce
1 teaspoon roasted sesame oil
2 tablespoons plus 1 teaspoon olive oil
1 tablespoon plus 1 teaspoon rice vinegar
Black pepper
2 tablespoons minced shallots

Preheat the oven to 400 degrees.

Heat the olive oil in a cast-iron skillet over high heat until hot, not smoking. Season the beef with salt and pepper to taste and sear it until dark brown on all sides. Place in the oven for 9 minutes. Allow to cool completely. Once the meat has cooled, slice it into 1/4-inch slices, then into thin strips. Place into a medium bowl and toss with the scallions.

To make the dressing, whisk together the ingredients. Pour over the beef and scallions and toss.

Serves 4

. . . .

Beef Salad

Spicy Pickapeppa sauce is available in specialty food shops.

2 teaspoons olive oil
1 beef tenderloin (about 1 pound)
Salt and black pepper
1 tablespoon chopped green bell pepper
1 tablespoon grated carrot
1 tablespoon finely chopped scallion

DRESSING
1 tablespoon yellow mustard
2 tablespoons prepared horseradish
2 teaspoons Worcestershire sauce
1 tablespoon mayonnaise
2 tablespoons sour cream
1 tablespoon olive oil
1 tablespoon red wine vinegar
1 teaspoon Pickapeppa sauce

Preheat the oven to 400 degrees.

Heat the olive oil in a cast-iron skillet over high heat until hot, not smoking. Season the beef with salt and pepper to taste and sear it until dark brown on all sides. Place it in the oven for 9 minutes. Remove it to a plate and allow to cool completely. Once the meat has cooled, slice it into 1/2-inch slices, then into 1/2-inch strips. Place into a medium bowl and toss with the green pepper, carrot, and scallion.

To make the dressing, whisk together the ingredients. Pour some of the dressing over the beef—you may not want to use all of it—and toss.

Serves 6

. . . .

Fresh Tuna Salad

1 lemon, cut into 8 wedges
4 celery stalks, halved
4 medium carrots, peeled and cut into 4 pieces each
10 black peppercorns
1 pound fresh tuna
1/2 cup plus 2 tablespoons chopped red onion
2 tablespoons capers, drained
1/4 cup plus 2 tablespoons mayonnaise
1/2 cup plus 2 tablespoons chopped sweet pickles
Freshly ground black pepper

Place the lemon, celery, carrots, and peppercorns in a large saucepan. Cover with cool water and bring to a boil. Add the fish and bring back to the boil. Turn off heat and allow to sit until cool, 1 to 1½ hours.

Drain and place the tuna in a bowl, then shred with a fork. Discard the lemon, celery, carrots, and peppercorns. Add the remaining ingredients and toss to mix well.

Serves 4

. . . .

Chipotle Chicken Salad

4 boneless and skinless chicken breasts
Salt and black pepper
1 tablespoon olive oil
1 canned chipotle pepper
¼ cup mayonnaise
¼ cup sour cream

Preheat the oven to 400 degrees.

Divide the breasts in half and sprinkle lightly with salt and pepper to taste. Heat the oil in a cast-iron skillet over high heat until hot, not smoking. Sear each breast until browned on both sides, about 2 minutes per side.

Place in the oven and bake for 5 minutes. Remove the chicken to a plate and allow to cool completely. Slice the breasts on the diagonal into ¼-inch slices and place in a mixing bowl.

Combine the chipotle pepper, mayonnaise, and sour cream in the bowl of a food processor and process until the pepper is finely minced. Spoon the dressing over the chicken and toss.

Serves 6

Traditional Chicken Salad.

Traditional Chicken Salad

4 boneless and skinless chicken breasts
Salt and black pepper
6 tablespoons olive oil
½ cup finely chopped sweet pickle
½ cup finely chopped canned pimiento
½ cup finely chopped celery
2 tablespoons finely chopped scallion
2 tablespoons balsamic vinegar

Preheat the oven to 400 degrees.

Divide the breasts in half and sprinkle lightly with salt and pepper to taste. Heat the oil in a cast-iron skillet over high heat until hot, not smoking. Sear each breast until browned on both sides, about 2 minutes per side.

Place in the oven and bake for 5 minutes. Remove the chicken to a plate and allow to cool completely. Slice the breasts on the diagonal into ¼-inch slices, then into chunks, and place in a mixing bowl.

Add the remaining ingredients to the chicken and toss well. Taste for salt and pepper.

Serves 6

Ham Salad

Mango chutney is available in specialty food shops, but you might want to substitute some other fruit chutney here.

3 pounds boneless ham steak
1 cup finely chopped onion
1 cup finely chopped celery
³/₄ cup finely chopped scallions
6 tablespoons finely chopped parsley
3 ounces cream cheese
3 ounces mango chutney

Preheat the broiler.

Broil the ham steak for 6 minutes on each side. Remove and allow to cool. Chop into bite-size pieces and place in a bowl.

Add the onion, celery, scallions, and parsley to the chopped meat and stir. Place the cream cheese and chutney in the bowl of a food processor and process until smooth. Stir into the salad.

Serves 6 to 8

. . . .

Pasta and Seafood Salad

¹/₂ pound tubettini pasta
1 tablespoon plus 1 teaspoon olive oil
1 lemon, cut into 8 wedges
3 garlic cloves, roughly chopped
2 cups cold water
³/₄ pound medium shrimp
³/₄ pound fresh tuna
1 large onion, roughly chopped
¹/₂ cup finely chopped scallions (green part only)
1 cup minced dill pickle

DRESSING
3 tablespoons olive oil
1 tablespoon red wine vinegar
1 teaspoon Dijon mustard
¹/₂ teaspoon salt
¹/₄ teaspoon black pepper

Cook the pasta according to package directions. Drain, then run the pasta under cold water and drain again thoroughly. Place in a large bowl and toss with 1 teaspoon olive oil.

Place the lemon and garlic in a saucepan and add the cold water. Bring to a boil, add the shrimp, and cook until the shrimp are bright pink, cooked through but still tender, about 3 minutes. Remove the shrimp to a colander with a slotted spoon and run them under cold water. Drain well. Peel and devein the shrimp and add them to the pasta.

Bring the cooking liquid back to a boil and add the tuna. Return to a boil, then turn off heat. Leave the tuna in the cooking liquid for 15 minutes, then remove it to a plate and let it cool.

Heat the remaining 1 tablespoon olive oil in a cast-iron skillet over medium-high heat until hot but not smoking. Add the onion and cook, stirring occasionally, until dark golden brown, 10 to 12 minutes. Set aside to cool.

Use a fork to shred the tuna. Add it, along with the onion, scallions, and pickle, to the pasta.

To make the dressing, combine the ingredients in a jar with a tight-fitting lid. Shake well. Pour the dressing over the salad ingredients and toss.

Serves 6

Refresh the shrimp by running them under cold water after cooking.

Seafood Shrimp Salad

1 lemon, cut into 8 wedges

3 garlic cloves, roughly chopped

2 cups cold water

1½ pounds medium shrimp

1½ pounds fresh tuna

2 generous tablespoons capers, drained

¼ cup coarsely chopped dill pickle

6 tablespoons chopped red onion

DRESSING

3 tablespoons minced red onion

3 tablespoons minced fresh dill

2 tablespoons minced dill pickle

3 tablespoons minced capers, plus 1 tablespoon brine

6 tablespoons olive oil

3 tablespoons red wine vinegar

1 teaspoon salt

¾ teaspoon black pepper

6 dashes Tobasco Sauce

Place the lemon and garlic in a saucepan and add the cold water. Bring to a boil, add the shrimp, and cook until the shrimp are bright pink, cooked through but still tender, about 3 minutes. Remove the shrimp to a colander with a slotted spoon and run them under cold water. Drain well. Peel and devein the shrimp and place them in a large bowl.

Bring the cooking liquid back to a boil and add the tuna. Return to a boil, then turn off heat. Leave the tuna in the cooking liquid for 15 minutes, then remove it to a plate and let it cool. Once cooled, flake the tuna and add it to the shrimp along with the capers, pickle, and onion.

To make the dressing, combine the ingredients in a jar with a tight-fitting lid. Shake well to combine. Pour the dressing over the salad ingredients and toss.

Serves 6

ABOVE: *Pasta and Seafood Salad.* BELOW: *Orzo and Vegetable Salad.*

ABOVE: *Macaroni and Cheese Salad.* BELOW: *Summer Pasta Salad.*

Salmon Salad

1 lemon, quartered

3 medium carrots, cut into rough pieces

4 celery stalks, cut into rough pieces

12 black peppercorns

3 to 4 cups cold water

1 pound salmon fillet, skin removed

2 tablespoons sour cream

3 tablespoons mayonnaise

3 tablespoons minced shallots

2 tablespoons finely chopped fresh dill

1/2 teaspoon grated lemon zest

1 teaspoon white wine vinegar

2 teaspoons capers, drained

2 tablespoons finely chopped scallion

1 hard-cooked egg, mashed

Place the lemon, carrots, celery, and black pepper-corns in a medium saucepan and add cold water. Bring to a boil over medium-high heat. Add the fish and bring it back to the boil. Turn off the heat and allow the fish to cool in the poaching liquid, 1 to 1½ hours. Combine the sour cream, mayonnaise, shallots, dill, lemon zest, vinegar, capers, scallion, and egg in a large bowl. Stir to combine. Flake the salmon into the dressing and toss gently.

Serves 4

Orzo and Vegetable Salad

1 pound orzo pasta

1/3 cup plus 2 tablespoons olive oil

1 large red bell pepper, cut into fine julienne

1 large red onion, diced

1 pound asparagus

1/2 cup chopped scallions

2 tablespoons raspberry vinegar

1/4 teaspoon salt

1/4 teaspoon black pepper

1 tablespoon minced shallot

1/4 cup freshly grated Parmesan cheese

Cook the orzo according to package directions. Drain, then run under cold water and drain again thoroughly. Place in a large bowl.

Heat 1 tablespoon olive oil in a large skillet over medium heat. Add the bell pepper and sauté until just tender, 3 or 4 minutes. Add to the orzo.

Heat 1 tablespoon olive oil in the same pan and add the onion. Sauté until translucent, 4 or 5 minutes. Add to the orzo.

Break off and discard the woody ends of the asparagus. Blanch the asparagus in boiling water until tender, about 4 minutes. Drain, run under cold water, and drain again. Dry the asparagus on paper towels, then cut on the diagonal into 1-inch pieces. Add them, along with the scallions, to the orzo and vegetables.

Make a vinaigrette by whisking the remaining 1/3 cup oil with the vinegar, salt, pepper, and shallots. Pour over the salad and toss. Add the Parmesan cheese and toss again.

Serves 6

OPPOSITE: *Place the salmon for the Salmon Salad in the hot poaching liquid.*

Macaroni and Cheese Salad

½ pound elbow macaroni
½ cup diced canned pimiento
1 cup grated Monterey Jack cheese
1 cup grated Cheddar cheese
1 large red onion, finely chopped
4 tablespoons olive oil
2 tablespoons red wine vinegar
1 teaspoon salt
½ teaspoon black pepper

Cook the elbows according to the package directions. Drain, run under cold water, and drain again thoroughly. Place in a large bowl.

Add the pimiento and Jack and Cheddar cheeses. Add the onion and toss.

Whisk together the oil, vinegar, salt, and pepper. Add to the salad and mix well.

Serves 6

Summer Pasta Salad

½ pound fusilli or rotelle pasta
¾ cup chopped dill pickle
½ cup chopped red onion
¼ cup chopped fresh dill
¼ cup mayonnaise
¼ cup sour cream
¼ teaspoon salt
⅛ teaspoon black pepper

Cook the pasta according to the package directions. Drain, run under cold water, and drain again thoroughly. Place in a large bowl.

Combine the remaining ingredients and stir well. Add to the pasta and toss.

Serves 6

Little Sa

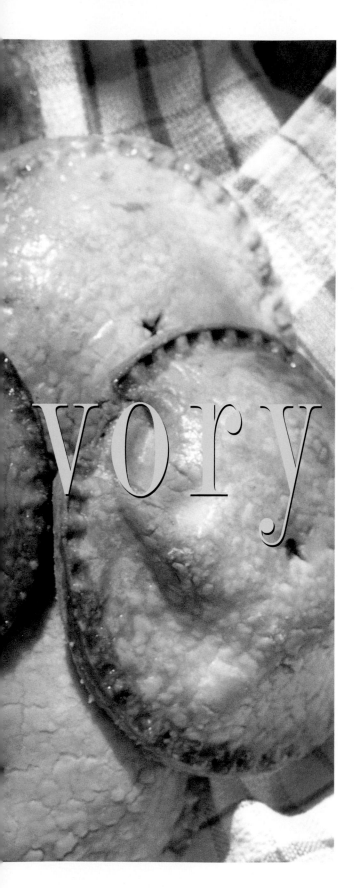

vory Pies

You will find versions of little savory pies in almost every national cuisine. I consider them among the neatest and easily packable of portable foods. These particularly invite experimentation, so once you get the hang of making them, don't hesitate to try your own versions.

Making Little Pies

Here's a master recipe for you to follow. These are especially easy to make with tart molds, called Tart Masters, which come in several sizes. They are available through Kitchen Connection, Inc., 8405 W. 45th Street, Lyons, IL 60534 (708-442-5232).

1 recipe pastry
1 recipe filling, at room temperature
1 egg, beaten

Divide the dough in half and roll out 1 piece to about ⅛ inch thick on a lightly floured board. Cut out 6 to 8 circles (depending on the recipe yield) about 3½ inches wide.

Spoon about 3 tablespoons of the filling into the center of the circle, mounding it up. Brush the edge of the circle lightly with beaten egg.

Roll out the remaining piece of pastry and cut out 6 to 8 more circles. Place these over the filling and press the edges to seal. Crimp the edges with a fork, and trim them with a sharp knife. Brush the tarts with the beaten egg, and use a skewer to poke a steam vent in the top of the tart. Alternatively, you can use a tart mold to seal and crimp the tarts.

Transfer the tarts to a baking sheet with a flat spatula and bake as directed. Cool them on a wire rack.

OPPOSITE: *Fillings for eight savory little pies.* TOP LEFT: *Mound filling onto pastry.* TOP RIGHT: *Brush the edge of the pastry lightly with beaten egg.* CENTER LEFT: *Place another circle of pastry over the filling.* CENTER RIGHT: *Seal the tart with a Tart Master.* BOTTOM LEFT: *The tart mold crimps the edges and pokes a steam vent.* BOTTOM RIGHT: *Before baking, brush the top of the tart with beaten egg.*

Hot Water Pastry

3/4 cup solid vegetable shortening
1/4 cup boiling water
1 tablespoon milk
1 teaspoon salt
2 cups all-purpose flour, or more as needed

Place the shortening in a bowl and pour the boiling water over it. Stir until smooth, then add the milk.

Combine the salt and flour in the bowl of a food processor, and pour the shortening mixture over the flour. Process until the dough forms a mass. Form into a ball, flatten slightly between 2 sheets of waxed paper or plastic wrap, and refrigerate for at least 1 hour.

Makes enough for 8 tarts

. . . .

Flaky Pastry

1 1/2 cups all-purpose flour
1/4 teaspoon salt
10 tablespoons (1 1/4 sticks) cold unsalted butter, roughly chopped
1/4 cup ice water

Place the flour and salt into the bowl of a food processor and pulse once or twice to mix. Add the butter and process only until it resembles coarse meal. Add the water and process just until the dough is formed into a ball. Remove and dust with flour if dough is sticky. Form the dough into 2 disks, wrap in plastic, and refrigerate for 1 hour.

Makes enough for 6 tarts

Cheese Pastry

2 cups all-purpose flour
Pinch of salt
1/2 cup cold unsalted butter, cut into bits
4 tablespoons cold solid vegetable shortening
2 cups grated Cheddar cheese
1/4 cup ice water

Toss the flour and salt together in a large bowl. Cut in the butter, shortening, and cheese with 2 knives or a pastry blender until the mixture resembles coarse meal. Stir in the water, mixing well but quickly. Form into 2 disks and wrap in plastic. Refrigerate for 30 minutes.

Makes enough for 8 tarts

. . . .

Vegetarian Filling

It's important to chop the vegetables fine for these little tarts.

1/4 cup olive oil
1/2 pound eggplant, peeled and cut into small dice
1/2 cup finely chopped onion
1/4 cup finely chopped red bell pepper
1/2 cup finely chopped zucchini
1 garlic clove, minced
1 tablespoon finely chopped fresh basil
1/4 teaspoon dried oregano
1/2 teaspoon salt
1/2 pound tomatoes (about 2 medium), peeled, seeded, and finely chopped

2 tablespoons minced parsley
2 tablespoons capers, drained
1 tablespoon fresh lemon juice
¹/₄ cup grated Parmesan cheese

Heat the olive oil in a large cast-iron skillet over moderately high heat. Add the eggplant, onion, red pepper, zucchini, garlic, basil, oregano, and salt. Toss to coat the vegetables with the oil. Cover and simmer over low heat for approximately 20 minutes, stirring occasionally, until the vegetables have softened. Add the tomatoes, increase the heat to medium-high, and cook uncovered, stirring occasionally, until the mixture has thickened. Remove from the heat and stir in the parsley, capers, lemon juice, and cheese. Allow to cool.

. . . .

ABOVE: *A finished Vegetarian Pie.* RIGHT: *Vegetarian filling.*

Preheat the oven to 425 degrees.

Prepare the tarts according to the master recipe (page 58). Bake for 30 minutes, or until the pastry is golden.

Makes enough for 10 tarts

Chicken Filling

1 tablespoon flour
1 large onion, finely diced
1 tablespoon olive oil
1 cup finely diced cooked chicken breast
³/₄ cup chicken stock
1 tablespoon minced capers
¹/₂ cup finely chopped toasted pecans
¹/₄ teaspoon black pepper

Heat a small cast-iron skillet over medium-high heat. Add the flour and cook, stirring occasionally with the edge of a metal spatula, until it begins to brown, 6 to 8 minutes. Do not let the pan get too hot. Remove from the heat and allow to cool.

Sauté the onion in the olive oil in a heavy skillet over medium-high heat until golden brown, 8 to 10 minutes, stirring occasionally. Add the chicken and stir to combine. Sprinkle in the browned flour and stir. Add the chicken stock and cook, stirring, until thickened, approximately 2 minutes. Stir in the capers, pecans, and pepper. Cool to room temperature.

Preheat the oven to 425 degrees.

Prepare the tarts according to the master recipe (page 58). Bake for 30 minutes, or until golden.

Makes enough for 8 tarts

ABOVE: *A finished Chicken Pie.* BELOW: *Chicken filling.*

Lamb Filling

½ cup chicken stock

2 tablespoons port wine

6 pitted prunes, finely chopped

½ pound boneless lamb, finely chopped

¼ teaspoon salt

⅛ teaspoon black pepper

1 tablespoon olive oil

1 small onion, finely chopped

2 garlic cloves, minced

½ cup finely chopped walnuts

Combine the chicken stock, port, and prunes in a bowl and set aside. Sprinkle the meat with salt and pepper and set aside.

Heat the oil in a heavy, medium skillet over moderately high heat. Add the onion and cook until it begins to brown, 4 or 5 minutes. Add the garlic and sauté for an additional minute. Remove from the pan and reserve. Add the meat to the same pan and cook over high heat until browned, approximately 2 minutes. Add the walnuts and cook for an additional minute. Add the chicken stock and prune mixture, and cook for a minute or so, stirring to loosen any browned bits on the bottom of the pan. Cook, stirring, until the mixture thickens, about 2 to 3 minutes. Cool to room temperature.

Preheat the oven to 425 degrees.

Prepare the tarts according to the master recipe (page 58). Bake for 30 minutes, or until golden.

Makes enough for 8 tarts

BELOW: *Lamb filling.* BOTTOM: *The finished Lamb Pie.*

Ham and Chicken Filling

1 tablespoon olive oil
1 boneless, skinless chicken breast
Salt and black pepper to taste
1 tablespoon flour
1 small boneless ham steak (6 ounces), finely chopped
1 cup toasted pecans, finely chopped
¹/₂ cup chicken stock
2 tablespoons Dijon mustard

Heat the oil in a small, heavy skillet. Sprinkle the chicken with salt and pepper to taste and cook until nicely browned, 2 to 3 minutes per side. Set aside to cool, then chop fine.

Heat a small cast-iron skillet over medium-high heat. Add the flour and cook, stirring occasionally with the edge of a metal spatula, until it begins to brown, 6 to 8 minutes. Do not let the pan get too hot. Remove from the heat and allow to cool.

Place the ham, chicken, and pecans in a large, heavy skillet and heat over medium-high heat until just heated through, about 2 minutes. Sprinkle with the browned flour and stir. Add the chicken stock and mustard and cook, stirring, until thickened, 3 or 4 minutes. Cool to room temperature.

Preheat the oven to 425 degrees.

Prepare the tarts according to the master recipe (page 58). Bake for 30 minutes, or until golden.

Makes enough for 8 tarts

ABOVE: *Ham and Chicken Pie.* BELOW: *Ham and Chicken filling.*

Oriental Beef Filling

1 tablespoon flour

1 tablespoon olive oil

1 boneless ribeye steak (6 ounces), all fat removed and finely chopped

3 large garlic cloves, minced

1 cup finely chopped scallions

1 tablespoon minced fresh ginger

¹/₂ cup chicken stock

1 tablespoon soy sauce

Heat a small cast-iron skillet over medium-high heat. Add the flour and cook, stirring occasionally with the edge of a metal spatula, until it begins to brown, 6 to 8 minutes. Do not let the pan get too hot. Remove from the heat and allow to cool.

Heat a large cast-iron skillet over medium-high heat. Add the olive oil and heat until hot. Add the beef and cook, stirring, until browned, 2 to 3 minutes. Add the garlic and cook for an additional minute. Add the scallions and ginger, and cook for

1 more minute. Sprinkle with the browned flour and stir. Add the chicken stock and soy sauce, and cook, stirring, until thickened. Cool to room temperature.

Preheat the oven to 425 degrees.

Prepare the tarts according to the master recipe (page 58). Bake for 30 minutes, or until golden.

Makes enough for 6 tarts

BELOW: *Oriental Beef filling.* BOTTOM: *The finished pie.*

Pork Filling

Make sure the potato is cut into very fine dice—no more than ¼ inch.

1 tablespoon flour
4 tablespoons olive oil
1 large onion, finely chopped
1 pork loin (12 ounces), all fat removed, finely chopped
½ teaspoon salt
¼ teaspoon black pepper
⅔ cup finely chopped scallions
1 cup chicken stock
1 large russet potato, peeled and finely diced

Heat a small cast-iron skillet over medium-high heat. Add the flour and cook, stirring occasionally with the edge of a metal spatula, until it begins to brown, 6 to 8 minutes. Do not let the pan get too hot. Remove from the heat and allow to cool.

Place the olive oil into a large, heavy skillet and heat over high heat. Add the onion and cook, stirring occasionally, until lightly browned, 4 to 5 minutes. Sprinkle the pork with the salt and pepper and add it to the onion. Cook until well browned, 3 to 4 minutes. Add the scallions and browned flour and cook, stirring, for 1 minute. Add the stock and cook, stirring from the bottom, until slightly thickened. Remove the pan from the heat and add the potato. Cool to room temperature.

Preheat the oven to 325 degrees.

Prepare the tarts according to the master recipe (page 58). Bake for 60 minutes, or until golden.

Makes enough for 8 tarts

Sausage and Cheese Filling

½ pound sweet Italian sausage, casing removed
2 tablespoons flour
6 tablespoons warm chicken stock
1 cup grated Monterey Jack cheese
1 Granny Smith apple

Heat a heavy, skillet over medium-high heat. Add the sausage and cook, stirring, until the meat is cooked through, about 5 minutes. Pour off the fat, return the pan to the heat, and sprinkle the meat with the flour. Cook, stirring, for about 1 minute. Add the chicken stock and cook, stirring, until thickened, about 4 minutes. Remove from the heat and cool to room temperature. Stir in the cheese.

Peel and core the apple. Cut it into thin (¼-inch) horizontal slices.

Preheat the oven to 425 degrees.

Prepare the tarts according to the master recipe (page 58), placing an apple round on the pastry before adding the filling. Bake for 30 minutes, or until the pastry is golden.

Makes enough for 6 tarts

Ham, Cheese, and Mustard Filling

Again, remember to keep the dice very small for these little pies.

1 boneless ham steak (12 ounces), finely diced
1 cup grated Monterey Jack cheese
Spicy brown mustard

Preheat the oven to 425 degrees.

Combine the ham and cheese in a bowl. Prepare the tarts according to the master recipe (page 58), placing a dollop of mustard on the pastry before adding the filling. Bake for 30 minutes, or until the pastry is golden brown.

Makes enough for 6 tarts

OPPOSITE: *Pork Pie.* ABOVE LEFT: *Sausage and Cheese filling.* ABOVE: *Ham, Cheese, and Mustard filling.*

Sandwic

h Spreads

All of these spreads can be used—separately or in combination—for tea sandwiches, which would be a perfect foil for soups and salads. But should you like sandwiches composed of many ingredients, use them as the basis for a

Dagwood-like construction. The spreads travel well, but my advice for making multilayer sandwiches portable is to individually wrap the ingredients, sliced and ready to use, then assemble the sandwich at your destination. Less chance of mishap that way.

Bean Spread

²/₃ cup Great Northern beans, soaked
Chicken stock
1 bay leaf
1 small onion, coarsely chopped
¹/₂ teaspoon raspberry vinegar
¹/₄ teaspoon black pepper
¹/₂ teaspoon Pickapeppa sauce

Drain the beans and rinse them under cool running water. Place them in a saucepan and cover them by about 1 inch with chicken stock. Add the bay leaf and bring to a boil over medium heat. Reduce the heat and simmer until the beans are tender. This should take from 1½ to 2 hours. Drain the beans, discard the bay leaf, and allow to cool.

Place the beans, onion, vinegar, pepper, and Pickapeppa sauce in the bowl of a food processor. Pulse until smooth, about 1 or 2 minutes.

Makes 2 cups

Smoked Trout Spread

1 smoked trout (7 ounces), skin removed
2 teaspoons fresh lemon juice
2 tablespoons prepared horseradish
1 tablespoon sour cream
1 teaspoon Worcestershire sauce
¹/₂ teaspoon Pickapeppa sauce
4 ounces cream cheese

Place all the ingredients in the bowl of a food processor fitted with the metal blade and mix until smooth, approximately 2 minutes.

Makes 1¹/₄ cups

Asiago and Red Pepper Spread

2 medium red bell peppers, roasted, peeled, and seeded

6 tablespoons cream cheese, softened

4 tablespoons minced shallots

½ teaspoon salt

½ teaspoon black pepper

½ cup grated Asiago cheese

Drain the roasted peppers well on paper towels. Place all ingredients except the Asiago cheese into the bowl of a food processor. Process until smooth, about 1 minute. Stir in the cheese.

Makes approximately 1¼ cups

Roasted Red Pepper and Boursin Spread

1 medium red bell pepper, roasted, peeled, and seeded

1 box (5.2 ounces) herbed Boursin cheese

2 tablespoons minced shallots

⅛ teaspoon salt

⅛ teaspoon pepper

Drain the roasted pepper well on paper towels. Combine pepper and the cheese in the bowl of a small food processor. Pulse for several minutes until well combined, scraping down the sides of the bowl. Stir in shallots, salt, and pepper.

Makes approximately ¾ cup

OPPOSITE: *The classic portable lunch: soup and sandwich.* ABOVE: *Tea sandwiches made with a variety of spreads.*

Olive and Sun–Dried Tomato Spread

1/4 cup pitted and roughly chopped oil–cured
   black olives
1/2 cup roughly chopped pimiento–stuffed
   green olives
1/2 cup roughly chopped sun–dried tomatoes
1/2 cup roughly chopped canned pimientos
3 tablespoons finely chopped parsley
2 anchovy fillets, mashed
2 teaspoons minced garlic
1/2 teaspoon dried oregano
1 teaspoon fresh lemon juice
1/2 teaspoon black pepper
4 ounces cream cheese, softened

Stir together all of the ingredients except the cream
cheese until well combined. Stir in the cream cheese
and mix until thoroughly blended.

Makes 1 1/2 cups

. . . .

OPPOSITE: *Two sandwich ideas.* TOP: *Trim the
crusts from a good thin-sliced bread and fill the sandwich with Refrigerator Wilted Onions (page 78).*
BOTTOM: *For a Dagwood, spread a soft roll with
Olive and Sun-Dried Tomato Spread (recipe this
page) and layer on wilted onions, ham, pickles, and
lettuce and tomato.*

Smoked Salmon Spread

3 ounces smoked salmon, roughly chopped
3 ounces cream cheese, softened
1 small onion, roughly chopped
1 tablespoon capers, drained

Place all the ingredients in the bowl of a food
processor. Process for several minutes until smooth.

Makes 1 generous cup

. . . .

Fresh Salmon Spread

1/2 cup Salmon Salad (page 54)
4 ounces cream cheese, softened
1 small onion, roughly chopped
6 dashes Tabasco sauce
1/2 teaspoon Worcestershire sauce

Place all the ingredients in the bowl of a food
processor. Process for several minutes until smooth.

Makes 1 generous cup

Pickles &

Relishes

I am sure that you have in your pantry
plenty of condiments, such as conventional
pickles and relishes, but I want to suggest
a few of my choice selections to add to
your recipe files. The caramelized onions
are a particular favorite.

Terrell's Pickles in a Hurry

5 Kirby cucumbers

5 fresh dill sprigs, or 1 teaspoon dried dill

3 garlic cloves, minced

³/₄ cup cider vinegar

¹/₃ cup coarse (kosher) salt

Pinch of dill seed

2 whole cloves

1 teaspoon pickling spices

1 teaspoon Tabasco sauce

2 bay leaves

12 black peppercorns

3 cups water

Wash the cucumbers and place them in a crock or glass bowl. Add the dill and garlic.

Place the remaining ingredients in a medium saucepan and bring them to a boil. Reduce the heat, cover, and simmer for 5 minutes. Remove from heat and allow to cool.

Pour this pickling liquid over the cucumbers. Submerge the cucumbers by weighting them with a plate and a heavy can. Cover the crock and refrigerate for 3 days.

Skim off any foam, slice the cucumbers, and store in a clean jar.

Makes 4 cups

. . . .

OPPOSITE: *Pickling spices for Terrell's Pickles in a Hurry.* ABOVE: *Spoon the sliced pickles into a jar through a wide-mouthed funnel.*

Caramelized Onions

1½ pounds small white onions
2 tablespoons unsalted butter
1 cup water
1 tablespoon sugar
1 tablespoon balsamic vinegar

Blanch the onions in rapidly boiling water to cover for 15 to 20 seconds, until the skins are loosened. Drain and run under cold water. Slice off a small piece from both ends and peel the onions. Cut an X in the root end of each onion to help keep the onions from separating while they cook.

Place the onions in a small saucepan with 1 tablespoon butter, the water, and the sugar. Bring to the boil. Reduce the heat and simmer for about 15 minutes, until the onions are tender and the liquid has evaporated. Add the remaining tablespoon of butter and the balsamic vinegar. Cook, stirring, until the onions are golden brown and slightly tacky to the touch.

Makes 2½ cups

Regrigerator-Wilted Onions

½ cup white vinegar
½ cup water
1 cup oil
⅛ teaspoon black pepper
½ teaspoon sugar
1 large onion, thinly sliced

Whisk together the vinegar, water, oil, pepper, and sugar.

Place the onion slices in a deep, narrow dish or measuring cup. Pour the liquid over the onion, cover, and refrigerate overnight.

Drain the onions before you serve them.

Makes 2½ cups

. . . .

Fresh Corn Relish

2 cups fresh corn kernels
2 tablespoons minced jalapeño pepper
½ cup finely chopped serrano pepper
½ cup diced red bell pepper
½ cup diced green bell pepper
2 tablespoons minced cilantro
1 tablespoon plus 1 teaspoon fresh lime juice
2 teaspoons olive oil
½ teaspoon salt
½ teaspoon black pepper

Combine the corn, jalapeño, serrano, bell peppers, and cilantro in a bowl. Stir. Drizzle the lime juice and olive oil over the mixture and sprinkle on the salt and pepper. Mix very well.

Makes 3½ cups

Tomato and Jalapeño Relish

**3 cups peeled, seeded, and chopped tomatoes
  (6 medium tomatoes)**
1½ teaspoons minced jalapeño pepper
1½ teaspoons minced serrano pepper
1½ cups chopped jicama
¾ cup roughly chopped onion
½ cup olive oil
¼ cup balsamic vinegar
½ cup fresh orange juice
1 teaspoon salt
½ teaspoon black pepper

In a medium mixing bowl, combine the tomatoes, jalapeño and serrano peppers, jicama, and onion. Stir.

Combine the oil, vinegar, orange juice, salt, and pepper in a jar with a tight-fitting lid. Shake well. Pour over the tomato mixture and stir. Taste and adjust the salt and pepper if necessary.

Makes almost 4 cups

Marinated Mushrooms

1 pound button mushrooms
2 teaspoons minced fresh oregano
1 teaspoon minced garlic
¼ cup plus 2 tablespoons red wine vinegar
1 cup olive oil
½ teaspoon salt
¼ teaspoon black pepper

Trim the ends of the mushrooms; wipe them clean with a damp paper towel if necessary. Cut each mushroom into quarters and place in a medium mixing bowl.

Whisk together the oregano, garlic, vinegar, oil, salt, and pepper in a bowl. Pour over the mushrooms and mix well. Allow to sit for at least 1 hour before serving.

Makes about 4 cups

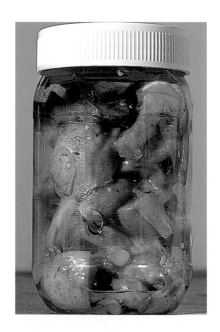

OPPOSITE: *Caramelized Onions.* ABOVE LEFT: *Tomato and Jalapeño Relish.* ABOVE: *Marinated Mushrooms.*

D

Cookies are probably the best example of a portable dessert. They are eminently packable and, besides, I've never met a person who didn't like them. Individual tarts are another good choice, as are

esserts

brownies and loaf cakes. And if you don't want to bother packing mixed fruit salad, there are always those individual, packed-by-nature desserts—apples and oranges. Fresh peaches and pears travel less well.

Shasta Mountain Brownies

6 ounces bittersweet chocolate

1/2 pound (2 sticks) unsalted butter

1/2 pound chocolate chip cookies (homemade if possible)

4 eggs

2 1/4 cups sugar

1 teaspoon vanilla extract

1 cup all-purpose flour

4 ounces pecans, chopped (1 cup)

Preheat the oven to 350 degrees. Lightly grease and flour two 9-inch square pans.

In a small bowl, melt the chocolate and butter together. (You can do this in a microwave or on the stove over a pot of simmering water.) Stir and set aside to cool slightly.

Place the cookies in the bowl of a food processor. Pulse to chop the cookies coarsely.

Combine the eggs, sugar, and vanilla in a large bowl. Beat with an electric mixer on medium speed until thick and lemon-colored, about 3 minutes. Add the melted chocolate and butter, and stir to combine. Mix in the flour gradually, just to incorporate. Fold in the chopped cookies and three quarters of the nuts.

Spread the batter in the 2 prepared pans and sprinkle with the remaining nuts. Bake approximately 40 minutes, or until set. The brownies will be soft in the center. Cool on a rack. Cut each pan of brownies into 9 pieces.

Makes 18 large brownies

Shasta Mountain Peanut Butter Cookies

½ cup unsalted butter, at room temperature

¼ cup granulated sugar, plus additional for rolling

1 cup dark brown sugar

1 cup chunky peanut butter

½ teaspoon vanilla extract

1 egg

2 ounces (⅓ cup) salted peanuts, chopped

1⅓ cups all-purpose flour

¼ teaspoon salt

½ teaspoon baking soda

In a mixing bowl, combine the butter, granulated sugar, brown sugar, and peanut butter. Beat with an electric mixer on medium speed until light and smooth, 3 to 4 minutes. Add the vanilla, egg, and peanuts, and stir until just combined.

Whisk together the flour, salt, and baking soda. Add all at once to the butter mixture. Stir until just combined. The dough will be stiff. Cover and refrigerate for at least 4 hours or overnight.

Preheat the oven to 350 degrees.

With your hands, shape 1½-tablespoon measures of the cookie dough (just smaller than golf balls) and roll in granulated sugar to coat. Place approximately 3 inches apart on a greased baking sheet and flatten with the bottom of a glass, then score crisscross with the tines of a fork.

Bake for 12 to 15 minutes, or until set and slightly golden. Allow to cool slightly on the baking sheet before removing. Cool on a rack.

Makes about 12 5-inch cookies

OPPOSITE: *Shasta Mountain Brownies.* BELOW: *Shasta Mountain Peanut Butter Cookies.*

Grandma Pleak's Icebox Cookies

4¹/₂ cups all-purpose flour

1 teaspoon salt

2 teaspoons baking soda

1 teaspoon ground cinnamon

¹/₂ teaspoon grated nutmeg

¹/₄ teaspoon ground cloves

1¹/₂ cups solid vegetable shortening, melted

1 cup packed dark brown sugar

1 cup granulated sugar

3 eggs

1 cup walnut or pecan halves

Whisk together the flour, salt, baking soda, cinnamon, nutmeg, and cloves. Set aside.

Combine the shortening and the sugars in a large bowl. Beat with an electric mixer on medium or low speed until well combined, 2 or 3 minutes. Add the eggs one at a time, beating after each addition. Add the flour mixture and mix on low speed just until dough forms. Stir in the nuts by hand.

Divide the dough into thirds. Place one third on a sheet of waxed paper and form into a rectangle, about 10 inches long, 2 inches wide, and 1½ inches high. Wrap with the waxed paper. Repeat with the other two pieces of dough and refrigerate overnight.

Preheat the oven to 375 degrees. Lightly grease 2 baking sheets.

Remove one log of the dough from the refrigerator and slice cookies approximately ¼ inch thick. Place cookies at least 1 inch apart on the prepared sheets. Bake for 9 to 10 minutes, until just browning yet still soft in the center. Remove from the oven and allow to cool slightly on the sheets before removing to wire racks to cool completely. Repeat with remaining dough. Store in an airtight container.

Makes about 72 cookies

. . . .

Pecan Coconut Biscotti

1 egg plus 1 egg white
½ cup vegetable oil
¾ cup sugar
1 teaspoon vanilla extract
½ teaspoon salt
¾ cup coarsely chopped pecans
½ cup sweetened flaked coconut
1½ cups all-purpose flour
1½ teaspoons baking powder

Combine the egg, egg white, and oil in a large bowl. Beat with an electric mixer on low speed until well combined. Add the sugar, vanilla, salt, pecans, and coconut and mix on low speed until completely blended, 1 or 2 minutes. Stir together the flour and baking powder in a small bowl. Add all at once to the egg mixture and mix on low speed until just combined. Cover with plastic wrap and refrigerate overnight.

Preheat the oven to 325 degrees. Lightly coat 2 baking sheets with vegetable spray.

Divide the dough into 2 balls. Place one ball of dough on each baking sheet. Flatten each ball into a long rectangle the length of the baking sheet and approximately 4 inches wide.

Bake for 30 minutes, or until crisp and lightly browned. Remove from the oven and allow to cool for several minutes. Using 2 large spatulas, carefully remove the baked dough from the sheets and place on a large cutting board. Cut each log on the diagonal into approximately 18 strips. Return the cookies to the baking sheets, laying the strips on their sides, and bake for 15 to 20 minutes, or until rich golden brown.

Makes approximately 36 biscotti

OPPOSITE: *Grandma Pleak's Icebox Cookies.*
ABOVE: *Pecan Coconut Biscotti.*

Lemon Crisps

1 cup blanched almonds
Zest of 1 lemon, cut into strips
½ cup unsalted butter, at room temperature
½ cup sugar
1 egg
1 tablespoon fresh lemon juice
1 teaspoon vanilla extract
½ cup sifted all-purpose flour

Preheat the oven to 375 degrees. Lightly grease 2
baking sheets.

Place the almonds on a baking sheet and bake
them, stirring occasionally, until golden brown,
about 10 minutes. Allow to cool.

Place the almonds and lemon zest in the bowl
of a food processor. Pulse until finely chopped.

Put the butter and sugar in a large bowl and
beat with an electric mixer on medium speed until
light and fluffy, about 3 minutes. Beat in the egg,
lemon juice, and vanilla. Add the almond-zest mixture and mix well. Add the flour and stir just to
combine.

Drop the dough by scant teaspoonfuls onto the
baking sheets and bake for about 12 minutes, until
the edges brown. Allow to cool slightly before trans-
ferring the cookies to a wire rack.

Makes 4 dozen cookies

Making Individual Tarts

Here's a master recipe for you to follow. I like these
sweet tarts best made with puff pastry, but you can
also use Hot Water Pastry or Flaky Pastry (page 60).
As with the savory pies, a tart mold (see page 58)
makes preparing these a breeze.

1 sheet store-bought puff pastry, cold but not frozen
  (see Note)
1 recipe filling, at room temperature
1 egg, beaten

N O T E : A 17½-ounce box of puff pastry contains
2 sheets. For best results, puff pastry should remain
cold. If the pastry starts to get soft and sticky, return
it to the refrigerator for a few minutes to firm it up
again.

Roll out the pastry to about ⅛ inch thick on a
lightly floured board. Cut out 12 rounds of pastry,
each about 3½ inches wide.

Spoon about 3 tablespoons of the filling into
the center of 6 of the rounds, mounding it up. Brush
the edge of the rounds lightly with beaten egg.

Place the remaining rounds over the filling and
press the edges to seal. Crimp the edges with a fork,
and trim them with a sharp knife. Alternatively, you
can use a tart mold to seal and crimp the tarts.
Brush the tarts with the beaten egg, and use a
skewer to poke a steam vent in the top of each tart.

Transfer the tarts to baking sheets with a flat
spatula and place them in the refrigerator for 30
minutes. Bake as directed. Cool on a wire rack.

Prune and Port Filling

1 cup fresh orange juice
$\frac{1}{2}$ cup plus 1 tablespoon port wine
$\frac{1}{2}$ cup finely diced pitted prunes
4 teaspoons sugar
2 teaspoons cornstarch
$\frac{1}{4}$ cup roughly chopped toasted pecans

Place the orange juice, $\frac{1}{2}$ cup port, prunes, and sugar into a medium saucepan over medium-high heat. Bring to the boil, reduce the heat, and simmer for 8 minutes. Allow to cool slightly. Combine the cornstarch with the remaining tablespoon port. Stir into the fruit mixture and return to the heat. Cook over medium-high heat, stirring constantly, until thickened, about 2 minutes. Stir in the chopped nuts. Set aside to cool completely.

Preheat the oven to 450 degrees.

Prepare the tarts according to the master recipe (page 86). Bake for 15 to 18 minutes, or until golden brown.

Makes 6 tarts

Peach and Port Filling

1 cup fresh orange juice
$\frac{1}{2}$ cup plus 2 tablespoons port wine
$\frac{1}{2}$ cup finely diced dried peaches
1 tablespoon plus 1 teaspoon sugar
2 teaspoons cornstarch
$\frac{1}{4}$ cup roughly chopped toasted walnuts

Place the orange juice, $\frac{1}{2}$ cup port, peaches, and sugar in a medium saucepan over medium heat. Bring to the boil. Reduce the heat and simmer for 8 minutes. Allow to cool slightly.

Combine the remaining 2 tablespoons port with the cornstarch. Stir into the fruit mixture and return to the heat. Cook over medium-high heat, stirring constantly, until thickened, about 2 minutes. Stir in the chopped nuts. Set aside to cool completely.

Preheat the oven to 450 degrees.

Prepare the tarts according to the master recipe (page 86). Bake for 15 to 18 minutes, or until golden brown.

Makes 6 tarts

OPPOSITE: *Lemon Crisps.* ABOVE LEFT: *Prune and Port Tart.* ABOVE: *Peach and Port Tart.*

Mixed Fruit Filling

1½ cups plus 2 tablespoons fresh orange juice
½ cup finely chopped mixed dried fruit
2 teaspoons cornstarch
¼ cup chopped toasted pecans

Place 1½ cups orange juice and the diced fruit in a medium saucepan over medium heat. Bring to the boil. Reduce the heat and simmer for 8 minutes. Allow to cool slightly. Combine the remaining 2 tablespoons orange juice with the cornstarch. Stir into the cooled fruit and return to the heat. Cook over medium-high heat, stirring constantly, until thickened, about 2 minutes. Stir in the chopped nuts. Set aside to cool completely.

Preheat the oven to 450 degrees.

Prepare the tarts according to the master recipe (page 86). Bake for 15 to 18 minutes, or until golden brown.

Makes 6 tarts

Apple and Cranberry Filling

1½ cups plus 2 tablespoons fresh orange juice
½ cup finely chopped dried apples
¼ cup dried cranberries
2 teaspoons cornstarch
¼ cup chopped toasted pecans

Place 1½ cups orange juice, the apples, and the cranberries in a medium saucepan. Bring to the boil. Reduce the heat and simmer for 8 minutes. Allow to cool slightly. Combine the remaining

2 tablespoons orange juice with the cornstarch. Stir into the fruit mixture and return to the heat. Cook, stirring, over medium-high heat until thickened, about 2 minutes. Stir in the chopped nuts. Allow to cool completely.

Preheat the oven to 450 degrees.

Prepare the tarts according to the master recipe (page 86). Bake for 15 to 18 minutes, or until golden brown.

Makes 6 tarts

Apple and Cherry Filling

1¹/₂ cups plus 2 tablespoons fresh orange juice
¹/₂ cup finely chopped dried apples
¹/₄ cup dried cherries
2 teaspoons cornstarch
¹/₄ cup chopped toasted pecans

Place 1½ cups orange juice, the apples, and the cherries in a medium saucepan. Bring to the boil. Reduce the heat and simmer for 8 minutes. Allow to cool slightly. Combine the remaining 2 tablespoons orange juice with the cornstarch. Stir into the fruit mixture and return to the heat. Cook, stirring, over medium-high heat until thickened, about 2 minutes. Stir in the chopped nuts. Allow to cool completely.

Preheat the oven to 450 degrees.

Prepare the tarts according to the master recipe (page 86). Bake for 15 to 18 minutes, or until golden brown.

Makes 6 tarts

. . . .

OPPOSITE TOP: *Apple and Cranberry Tart.*
OPPOSITE BOTTOM: *Mixed Fruit Tart.* ABOVE:
Apple and Cherry Tart.

Fresh Fruit Salad.

Bourbon Almond Loaf

1 cup blanched almonds
1 cup sifted all-purpose flour
¾ teaspoon baking powder
¼ teaspoon salt
¼ cup bourbon
¼ cup water
⅓ cup unsalted butter, at room temperature
1 cup sugar
6 tablespoons egg white (about 4)

Preheat the oven to 375 degrees. Lightly grease and flour an 8½ × 4½-inch loaf pan.

Place the almonds on a baking sheet and toast in the oven, stirring occasionally, until golden brown, about 10 minutes Allow to cool. Place the almonds in the bowl of a food processor and pulse until coarsely ground.

Whisk together the almonds, flour, baking powder, and salt.

Combine the bourbon and water.

Place the butter and sugar in a large bowl. Beat with an electric mixer at medium speed until light and fluffy, about 3 minutes. Add the dry ingredients alternately with the liquid, beginning and ending with the dry and beating well after each addition.

Beat the egg whites until stiff. Gently fold into the batter. Pour the batter into the pan and bake for 1 hour, or until a cake tester comes out clean. Cool on a rack.

Makes 1 loaf

Fresh Fruit Salad

2 medium navel oranges
1 cup seedless grapes, cut into halves
1 cup blueberries
2 cups cantaloupe or honeydew melon chunks
½ cup fresh orange juice
Sugar to taste

Peel the oranges. Plunge into boiling water for 30 to 45 seconds, remove from the water, and using a sharp paring knife, scrape off any white pith. Slice along the membranes with a sharp knife to remove the orange sections, then cut the sections in half.

Combine oranges with the remaining ingredients and toss well.

Serves 6

Mashed Pear Cake

3 pears, peeled, cored, and cut into chunks
1/3 cup water
1/4 cup granulated sugar
2 tablespoons Poire William (pear liqueur)
1 1/2 cups sifted all-purpose flour
1/4 teaspoon salt
1 scant teaspoon baking soda
1 teaspoon freshly grated nutmeg
1/2 cup unsalted butter, at room temperature
1/2 cup packed brown sugar
1 egg

Preheat the oven to 350 degrees. Grease and lightly flour an 8½ × 4½-inch loaf pan.

Place the pears, water, and granulated sugar in a medium, heavy saucepan over medium heat. Cook until the water evaporates and the pears begin to caramelize, about 10 minutes. Mash the pears and stir in the Poire William.

Whisk together the flour, salt, baking soda, and nutmeg.

Combine the butter and brown sugar in a large bowl. Beat with an electric mixer on medium speed until light and fluffy, about 3 minutes. Beat in the egg.

Gently stir in the dry ingredients until just combined. Fold in the pears. Pour the batter into the pan and bake for 1 hour, or until a cake tester comes out clean. Cool on a rack.

Makes 1 loaf

Espresso Chocolate Loaf with Walnuts

2 ounces bittersweet chocolate
1 1/2 cups sifted all-purpose flour
1 1/2 teaspoons baking powder
1/4 teaspoon baking soda
1/4 teaspoon salt
1 tablespoon instant espresso granules
1/3 cup unsalted butter, at room temperature
3/4 cup sugar
2 eggs
1/2 cup buttermilk
1 cup chopped walnuts

Preheat the oven to 350 degrees. Lightly grease and flour an 8½ × 4½-inch loaf pan.

Place the chocolate in a bowl set over a pot of simmering water and melt (or melt in a microwave oven). Remove from the heat and allow to cool.

Whisk together the flour, baking powder, baking soda, salt, and espresso granules.

Place the butter and sugar in a large bowl and beat with an electric mixer on medium speed until light, about 3 minutes. Beat in the chocolate. Beat in the eggs, one at a time.

Stir in the buttermilk, then add the dry ingredients, stirring until just combined. Gently fold in the nuts. Pour the batter into the pan and bake for 1 hour, or until a cake tester comes out clean. Cool on a rack.

Makes 1 loaf

Equipment

Personally, I'm always squirreling away containers other food has come in, so I have them to use to give leftovers to a guest without worrying whether or not the container is returned. But these also work fine for single servings of portable food.

For larger quantities and more formal transporting of food, though, you should invest in sturdy stackable containers.

The rectangular shapes are ideal for sandwiches and cookies and muffins; spreads, pickles, and relishes fit neatly into the cylinders. You can find good quality, inexpensive casseroles with lids. Thermal carafes, like the one at right from A. K. Das, are ideal for transporting hot or cold soups, but room temperature soups can go in simple quart bottles with pop tops. And I think you should invest in a couple of funnels—including a wide-mouthed one.

Look for sturdy containers with good solid seals; you want something that will be airtight. And you know my thoughts about decorator colors— they send me running for the hills. Don't ever settle for one of those nasty noncolors; stick to white or black or dark green.

Index

"Lee Bailey understands the head-long pace of modern life but never quite forgets the hunger for what was best of our past." —FOOD & WINE

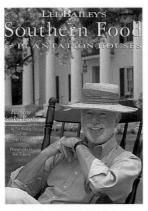

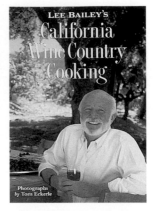

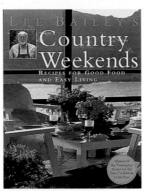
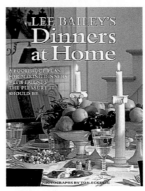
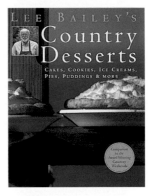

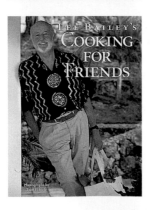

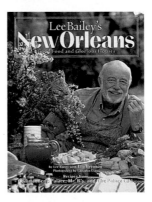